ME

A Book of Prayers
to Comfort Dying Persons
and Their Loved Ones

by Maureen Rinella

Abbey Press
St. Meinrad, IN 47577

© 1997 Maureen Rinella
Published by One Caring Place
Abbey Press
St. Meinrad, IN 47577
1-800-325-2511
Call for complete catalog of publications.

Library of Congress Catalog Number
97-73788

ISBN
0-87029-304-4

Book design by Scott Wannemuehler

Printed in the United States of America

Table of Contents

Acknowledgements

I owe a special gratitude to three earth-angels who guided and encouraged me through this project:

To Donna Stone, R.N., a dear friend, a deeply spiritual person, and a hospice nurse who became my soul mate in the writing of this book. Donna's enthusiasm and spiritual insights provided a gentle yet powerful touch in the shaping of this work.

To Marsha Weber, a long-time friend, a librarian, and a professional writer whose letters of praise and encouragement became the fuel that fed the fire within me.

To Carole Webb, R.N., my friend who has worked in intensive care; I thank you for reading my work and for encouraging me to believe in myself and remain focused on my goal through the difficult times.

Thanks to my parents, Gerald and Evelyn Fitzpatrick, who instilled in me the importance of faith and trust in a loving God.

Thanks to Sister Daniel Therese Coyle, Julia Rayl, Virginia Buchfinck, and to my many friends in Baker City and Portland, Oregon, who encouraged me and prayed for me.

A special thanks to my dear husband, Larry, and our three sons, James, Dan, and David, who continually add inspiration and dimension to my life.

*Dedicated with love
in memory of my dear niece,
Julie Ann Sanders,
whose beauty shines forever.*

Introduction

This book focuses on the spiritual needs of those who are near death. The prayers are written in the first person and speak directly out of the experience of the dying person. The book can therefore be used as a source of comfort and inspiration by a person near death, depending on his or her health and abilities.

Just as often, it will be used by a loved one or caring professional who wishes to become a compassionate messenger of hope to the person who is facing death. The prayers and Scripture passages can be read aloud for the benefit of the dying person. Such a reading will also bring comfort to friends and loved ones who may be near at hand as the time of death approaches.

Most people don't know what to say or do when someone they know and love is facing death. To be able to be helpful at a time when one feels powerless can relieve some of the anxiety and pain of being with a loved one at this challenging time. This book makes that possible.

Why I Wrote This Book

My personal call is to be a spiritual advocate for and to dying persons. My journey took me to a nursing home in a small town in northeastern Oregon where I volunteered to be a friend and support person to those who were dying alone and lonely. As death approached, I stayed with them, prayed with them, and shared my cup of hope with them. I have sat and prayed through more dyings than I can count, yet there were many more who died alone.

My search for appropriate prayers that spoke to the specific issues that face dying persons took me to the back shelves of used-book stores, where I discovered a wealth of soul-stirring language that was filled with joy and hope in the face of death. The prayers in an old Lutheran prayer book, John Frederick Starck's *Daily Handbook*, first published in German in 1728 and translated into English in 1904, became my most valuable tool to stir the flames of faith and hope in the souls of dying people. They are at the heart of this book.

However, the language of the prayers was in many cases archaic and difficult to read. I have therefore reworked the prayers, simplifying them and adding my own inspiration to them. I have designed them to be non-denominational Christian prayers based on the promises of Scripture.

I have maintained much of the traditional flavor of the prayers because I believe that in this way they will be of greater comfort and familiarity to many of those who are dying.

In an age that threatens to erode the dignity of the end of life, it is my hope that the prayers will be of comfort and inspiration to a wide range of people. They are for churchgoers as well as those who have stopped going or have never gone.

Because they are written in the first person, they are particularly powerful in helping a dying person establish an intimacy with the merciful Giver of Life who is calling the person home.

My hope is that, through this book, a dying person will be able to envision death as part of the ultimate journey of the soul.

I also hope that the book will help those who accompany a dying person to offer a companion's loving, supportive, and strong hand of faith as the dying person undertakes the final journey home—may it be a journey filled with dignity and peace.

Structure of the Book

The book is divided into two main parts, along with the Introduction, Postscript, and Appendix.

Part One, "The Soul's Journey Home," contains prayers and Scripture passages arranged in three sections. Section I, "Prayers for Terminally Ill Persons," consists of a series of meditations that relate to many of the spiritual issues faced by someone who is terminally ill.

Section II, "Scripture Passages and Prayers to Comfort Dying Persons," will be of great comfort in the final weeks and days. The Scripture passages in this section, when read alone, are filled with the promise of hope and joy, and are appropriate at any time. The prayers can also be read independently, without the Scripture passages, as one continuous prayer.

The prayers in Section III, "Prayers for the Final Hours," focus on final concerns about the afterlife. The aim is to

foster a tender and comforting intimacy
between the dying person and God at a
time when physical difficulties may be at
their height. As death arrives, the closing
"Holy, Holy" acknowledges the Holy
Presence that fills the room.

Part Two, "Reflections of Hope,"
offers stories and meditations that come
from my own experience with death and
loss. It is my hope that they may prove
uplifting and helpful to readers who
want to reflect on the profound meaning
of death, a subject we too often avoid.
The reader who is going to be a companion to a dying loved one is encouraged to
look at this material early on. It should
prove helpful and reassuring as the reader encounters the mystery of death.

Finally, a brief poem I wrote on the
death of my grandfather appears as a
Postscript, and an Appendix offers sug-
gestions of how a care-giving friend or
loved one can offer physical, emotional,
and spiritual comfort and support to a
person who is dying.

How to Use This Book

When accompanying a dying person, pray for guidance from the Holy Spirit. Ask that God use your voice, your touch, your compassion, and your faith as channels of Divine Love and Presence.

Convey the calm assurance that God loves the suffering person, is with that person, has always been with that person, and will not abandon the person in this time of need. Nor will you.

When a person is in the final stage of dying, sit close to her, with your hand touching her if possible. Read the prayers aloud, in a gentle voice. Read them slowly and reverently, realizing that these prayers may be the last prayers of the dying person, and that they are heard by a loving God who is very close to the person's suffering and dying.

It is possible to bring a message of hope and spiritual comfort to a loved one during the final months, weeks, days, and hours of his or her life. The message of this book is a simple one: the body may be dying, but the soul is not. The promise of eternal salvation is the hope that transcends all fear—especially the fear of the unknown that so often accompanies death.

This book is not only about dying, but also about living and loving. May it help you cross the line of fear when you hear a dying person cry, "Be with me!" Your loving comfort, support, and encouragement can help sustain your dying loved one until the Heavenly Creator calls, "Be with Me!" for eternity.

Part One

The Soul's Journey Home

I: Prayers for Terminally Ill Persons

Are any among you suffering? They should pray.

—James 5:13

In times of fear and doubt, it gives strength to the soul to focus on all that is ours because of God's love. What sweeter or more pleasant vision could any dying person bring before his mind than that of the joys of heaven?

Meditation on Heaven

LORD, GOD OF HOSTS, my soul longs for you. When will I see your face and stand before your throne in the company of all the angels and the believers who have gone before me? What glory and happiness will be mine when I have been parted from my body and have fallen asleep in Christ! I will be filled with peace, crowned with glory and honor, and live forever in Heavenly splendor. What glory and joy wait for me when I will see our Almighty God face to face!

All that I here believed, I there will see. What I could not understand here, I will know and understand there. There I will be filled with a Heavenly light. What joy it will be to behold the great and glorious God in all God's majesty! There I will meet my dear ones and friends who have died before me; and I will be with them in the sweetest relationship forever. All of my hopes will be realized; I will always be with my Lord; no sorrow will ever touch me. And all this will not be for only an hour, or a year, but without ceasing, forever and ever. Amen.

Thoughts of God's presence with us when we suffer are comforting to the soul. Though sight, hearing, and all the senses may fail, the dying one can depend on the promise, "I will be with you in times of trouble," and believe this promise will be fulfilled in the hour of death.

Prayer for God's Help

LORD JESUS come, take my soul into Heavenly glory. I long and thirst for the fullness of Heaven. I am not alarmed by the thought of death, for I die in the love of my Heavenly Creator. The one who through all my life has sustained, nourished, led, and guided me will not leave me when the end of my life approaches. God's great love for me will not permit this to happen.

I am not afraid of death; for I die united with Jesus Christ. He has said, "I am with you always, even unto the end

of the world," and he will be with me in
death. Just as he loved me enough to die
for me, his great love for me will be with
me when I am about to die.

The Holy Spirit has consecrated my
body in this life, and will remain united
with me in death, to bear witness with
my spirit that I am certainly God's child.
Though my speech should fail me and
deprive me of the power to pray, the
Spirit will intercede for me with groanings which cannot be uttered. The Holy
Spirit already assures me that I am an
heir of Heaven and will enter upon its
full possession. Amen.

*When the dying person looks back
upon his whole life, he sees the goodness
of God in it all. Whatever good there is in
us is God's work. Whatever earthly possessions we have are God's gift. God's tender mercy and goodness endure forever.*

Meditation on God's Goodness
ETERNAL AND HOLY CREATOR, I

have experienced your loving kindness.
It has been with me every hour, every
day, every week, every year. In my child-
hood, your mercy took me in its arms
like a mother and nourished me. In my
youth, your goodness took me by the
hand and accompanied me everywhere.
And in my later years, your loving kindness provided for me, preserved me, sustained me, and showered many blessings
upon me.

In your mercy you have filled my soul
with Heavenly light, illumined me by
your Word, sanctified me by your Holy
Spirit, and brought me to true and living
knowledge of you. Let your mercy and
faithfulness be with me till death, till my
soul returns to you for rest.

For all the goodness you have given to
me, I give you thanks. Good and merciful
God, I praise you now and through eternity. Amen.

*Impatience is difficult to overcome. It
does not make the cross lighter, only*

*heavier. Through prayer we ask God to be
with us in our suffering. And we pray to
the Holy Spirit to comfort us with the
knowledge that we are not abandoned by
God, and that in God's time this cross
will be lifted.*

Prayer for Patience and Strength

LORD JESUS, all my desire is before
you. I need your grace to help me bear
my cross. Dearest God in Heaven, I need
the gift of patience. With your help and
strength I can bear and endure all. Do
not let the burden become too heavy for
me, nor the trial too great.

Have patience with my weakness,
Dear Savior. Give me the assurance of
your precious love that my sufferings will
last for only a short time. Do not let my
cross drive your Word from my heart, nor
weaken my faith, nor stop my prayers.
Give me new strength and new courage
when I must weather a new storm, or
have just passed through one.

Strengthen me with your grace, that

my tears be a seed from which good fruit
will grow. Jesus, Lord of Mercy, I pray
that the thorns which have pierced me
will bear roses.

*The full awareness of relationships is
never more clear than in the face of
death. We can trust in the faithfulness of
God. We will be together again. We can
give our dying loved ones permission to
continue their journey without us. And
we can pray with them for our well-being
after they are gone. The ties of love—the
sweetest of God's gifts that bind us to one
another—are strengthened, not severed by
death.*

Prayer of Farewell to Dear Ones
ETERNAL, GRACIOUS, AND
MIGHTY GOD, I do not know how near
the end of my life may be; therefore, I
desire to prepare myself for death while I
have this time. I look with joy to Heaven
where my Heavenly Creator waits to
receive me. I am filled with happiness as

I anticipate my reunion with my friends and dear ones who have gone before me.

Lord, I thank you for all the joys of my life, especially for the people you have given to me to love and those who have loved me and helped me in my journey of life. Almighty God, I commend them to your protection, love, and grace. Bless them for the love and kindness which they have shown me. Keep them in faith and in holiness, that we may see one another in Heaven. I go before them, but in Heaven those who believe and are children of God will meet again.

Faithful God, pour your abundant blessing upon those whom I leave behind me, and whom my departure will grieve and pain. I have blessed them; let them be blessed. Amen.

It is not easy to forgive, but as we strive for this, we keep in mind that we are forgiven first by our forgiving God. Forgiveness brings an infusion of light into the desolation of interior darkness. It

*brings peace of heart. It cleanses the soul
with the soothing balm of divine grace
and prepares us to meet God face to face.*

Prayer for Forgiveness

MERCIFUL AND LOVING CRE-
ATOR, I do not know when my life will
end. I desire that when my time comes, I
may leave the world at peace with all
people. I desire to free my heart of all
anger, and I willingly forgive and ask forgiveness, in order that you may receive
me into Heaven.

I forgive from my heart all those who
have at any time offended me by words
or actions. I forgive them, not only with
my mouth but also with my heart, and
before God. I will not think of their
offenses anymore; I will let them go.

Merciful God, graciously forgive me
all the sins which I have committed out
of malice or weakness, intentionally or
unintentionally, against all whom I have
associated with in my life.

Heavenly Creator, have mercy on me.

Jesus, wash me clean from all my sins
and intercede for me. Holy Spirit, sancti-
fy my heart and cleanse it from all
imperfections. To your holy name be
glory, honor, and praise now and ever-
more. Amen.

*As we approach death, we often have
many things to arrange. We want to put
our house in order, and in our anxiety to
do this we sometimes forget the most
important thing of all: the care of the
soul. Let us daily commit both body and
soul to God's keeping, now and at the
hour of our death.*

Prayer Commending the Soul to God

GRACIOUS AND LOVING CRE-
ATOR, I commend myself to you and
commit my soul with all its powers to
your keeping. Free my heart from all
worldly things, that I may delight in you
alone.

Fill my heart with your Holy Spirit.
Help me to remember Jesus Christ and

to keep his atoning death before my eyes.

When the hour of my death is near, be with me. If I should lose my speech, let me taste your sweetness in my heart, and feel your presence there. I pray for the grace to die happy and joyful.

As my spirit leaves my body, I commend it to you; take it into your hands. Into your hands I commit my soul. Receive my spirit and lead it into the joys of Heaven like a bride to the wedding festivities, like a child to its inheritance.

II: Scripture Passages and Prayers to Comfort Dying Persons

Let anyone who is thirsty come to me, and let the one who believes in me drink. As the scripture has said, "Out of the believer's heart will flow rivers of living water." —John 7:37-38

Isaiah 49:15-16 *...I will not forget you. See, I have inscribed you on the palms of my hands.*

Loving and merciful God, you have created me, blessed me, loved me, and sustained me all of my life; help me in my sufferings and in my hour of death. Blessed Holy Spirit, strengthen me and keep me strong in my faith. Fill my heart with the fire of your love, and enlighten me to life eternal. I place my trust in the King of Divine Mercy; for God I live, for God I die.

John 8:12 *Again Jesus spoke to them, saying, "I am the light of the world. Whoever follows me will never walk in darkness but will have the light of life."*

Jesus, you are the Light of my soul. When my eyes become darkened, let the Heavenly glory arise in my soul. Do not leave me when my sight fails, but show me your blessed image upon the cross.

Though I walk through the valley of the shadow of death, I will fear no evil because you are with me. Remain with me, strengthen me, and let me be your own, here in time and there in eternity.

Psalm 40: 17 *As for me, I am poor and needy, but the Lord takes thought for me. You are my help and my deliverer; do not delay, O my God.*

Jesus, I trust in you from the depths of my soul. Come and release me. Give to my body its rest and take my soul to your eternal joys in Heaven. You have so often comforted me in my sadness, cheered me in suffering, refreshed me in trouble, and sustained me under the cross, and I believe you are with me as the end of my life approaches. Open to me now the door to Heaven and eternal life.

Isaiah 41:10 *Do not fear, for I am with you, do not be afraid, for I am* *your God. I will strengthen you, I will help you, I will uphold you with my victorious right hand.*

Jesus, you are my only Intercessor with your Heavenly Father. You sit at the right hand of God and plead for us. Blessed Holy Spirit, my Comforter in trouble, be with me with your consolation to my end. I have powerful help; for my God is with me, and God's angels surround me. I will die with the peace of Jesus Christ overflowing in my soul.

Psalm 73: 23-24 *Nevertheless I am continually with you; you hold my right hand. You guide me with your counsel, and afterward you will receive me with honor.*

Dearest Jesus, when my death struggle begins, help me to wrestle and overcome. By your power and the grace of your Holy Spirit I will be faithful unto death. I will not leave you; you are the Friend of my soul. Good Shepherd, protect me; you are my delight and the

Bridegroom of my soul. Lead me out of sorrow to joy. Fill my heart with the glorious hope of eternal salvation.

Psalm 17:15 *As for me, I will behold your face in righteousness; when I awake I will be satisfied, beholding your likeness.*

Lord Jesus, my soul is glad when I think of your glory and of the happiness which you have prepared for me. I leave the world willingly, because I am going to my Lord, my Savior and Redeemer. My sweetest delight will be to see the perfection of beauty, truth, wisdom, love, compassion, and mercy that is reflected in your beloved face. I desire to adore you, praise you, and worship you eternally.

Heb. 5:9 *And having been made perfect, he became the source of eternal salvation to all those who obey him.*

I know that when I pass from this world, I will leave sorrow behind me and come into the presence of God. I'll pass from burdens to pleasure, from anxiety to peace, from labor to rest, from sorrow to joy. My soul rejoices. Loving Creator, here I am; take my soul, glorify it, receive it into Heaven. My Jesus, I am yours and you are mine; in life and in death we will remain inseparable.

2 Cor. 5:1 *For we know that if the earthly tent we live in is destroyed, we have a building from God, a house not made with hands, eternal in the heavens.*

Loving Creator, King of grace and mercy, you have prepared for me many and glorious gifts in Heaven. And because death will open to me the door to this glory, I am not afraid. If an earthly king can adorn his palace so beautifully that we are filled with wonder when we behold it, how great and glorious must be the splendor of the Heavenly King! I look with joy to Heaven; for my home is there.

Isaiah 35:10 *And the ransomed of the Lord will return, and come to Zion with singing; everlasting joy will be upon their heads; they will obtain joy and gladness, and sorrow and sighing will flee away.*

Remember, Jesus, that I am redeemed with your precious blood. Let me soon enter into your Heavenly Zion. I have eaten the bread of sorrow; let me soon eat the bread of Heaven, the food of angels. Fill me with joy and gladness. Let my soul have a vision of your glory. Lighten my sufferings and refresh me, in and through you, eternally.

2 Tim. 4:7-8 *I have fought the good fight, I have finished the race, I have kept the faith. From now on there is reserved for me the crown of righteousness, which the Lord, the righteous judge, will give me on that day, and not only to me but also to all who have longed for his appearing.*

Jesus, help me to overcome when the final struggle begins. Stand by me and give me the victory. Help me in my distress and weakness. Let your grace strengthen me. After the fight, the crown; after the battle, the victory! How gloriously I will be adorned and crowned by you after my death. Show me the crown which you have prepared for me, and fill my soul with your gracious presence.

Rev. 2:10; 3:5 *Do not fear what you are about to suffer.... If you conquer, you will be clothed like them in white robes, and I will not blot your name out of the book of life; I will confess your name before my Father and before his angels.*

By faith I see your majesty and glory, and the splendor in which you dwell; and I see the angels, and all the faithful who have ever lived on earth, standing around your throne, praising you, and saying, "Holy, Holy, Lord God of Hosts."

By faith I see myself standing in their midst after I have calmly and peacefully departed from this world. I will wear a glorious crown upon my head, be clothed with white robes, and shine like the sun.

Romans 8:38-39 *For I am convinced that neither death, nor life, nor angels, nor rulers, nor things present, nor things to come, nor powers, nor height, nor depth, nor anything else in all creation, will be able to separate us from the love of God in Christ Jesus our Lord.*

You, Jesus Christ, are the Sustainer of life. I will not die even though I cease to breathe; for I live in you, and you in me. My life in you will now become perfect. I will live in your presence eternally, and neither things present nor things to come will be able to separate me from you. You are the way. Lead me through the dark valley of death to eternal life.

James 1:12 *Blessed is anyone who*

endures temptation. Such a one has stood the test and will receive the crown of life that the Lord has promised to those who love him.

Lord Jesus, give me patience and strength. I give you my body and soul. By your great mercy and grace, bring me to eternal life and joy. My Savior and Redeemer, receive the soul that waits for you. How I long to see God's face, to be with the angels and saints in Heaven, and to walk in Heavenly brightness and glory.

Psalm 31:5 *Into your hand I commit my spirit; you have redeemed me, O Lord, faithful God.*

Gracious and loving God, I commend myself to you and commit my soul with all its powers to your keeping. Free my heart from all worldly things that I may delight in you alone. Fill my heart with your Holy Spirit.

Help me to remember Jesus Christ, and to keep his all-atoning death before my eyes. Receive the dove that flies to you for safety. Let your angels guard me and protect me.

Heb. 12:22-23 *But you have come to Mount Zion and to the city of the living God, the Heavenly Jerusalem, and to innumerable angels in festal gathering, and to the assembly of the firstborn who are enrolled in heaven, and to God the judge of all, and to the spirits of the righteous made perfect.*

My Jesus, how glorious will be the vision when I behold you in your glory amid the throng of angels and saints in Heaven! I rejoice when I think of it. I will leave the earth, but I will enter into glory; I will leave my sorrows, but I will enter into gladness; I will leave my loved ones, if only for a while, but I will enter into the company of the holy angels.

John 10:27-28 *My sheep hear my voice. I know them, and they follow*

*me. I give them eternal life, and they
will never perish. No one will snatch
them out of my hand.*

Jesus, my Good Shepherd, bring me,
your poor sheep, into the blessedness of
Heaven. Protect me in my final battle.
Take my soul, like a weary lamb, into
your arms and lift it to Heaven. I am
safe with Jesus, my Guide and Savior.

Rev. 14:13   *And I heard a voice from
heaven saying, "Write this: Blessed
are the dead who from now on die in
the Lord." "Yes," says the Spirit, "they
will rest from their labors, for their
deeds follow them."*

Dearest Savior, give to my soul the
comforting assurance that I die in you.
You have lived in me, and I in you; therefore I desire to die in you, in your love, in
your sacred wounds, in your grace. Sweet
Jesus, hear me, release me, and bring me
into your glory eternally.

2 Tim. 4:18   *The Lord will rescue me*

*from every evil attack and save me
for his Heavenly kingdom. To him be
the glory forever and ever. Amen.*

Almighty God, remember me in
mercy, and have compassion upon me.
Give me a quiet and gentle end. The day
of my death is my day of redemption,
and the hour of my death is the hour
when I enter into eternal joy. And now,
through a blessed death, deliver me from
all evil and bring me into glory.

Matt. 25:34 *Then the King will say
to those on his right hand, "Come,
you who are blessed by my Father,
inherit the kingdom prepared for you
from the foundation of the world."*

Dearest Jesus, when I part from my
body, let me hear your welcome words:
"Come, you who are blessed of my
Father." And on the last day let my body
and soul inherit an eternal kingdom. I
cling to you by faith, confident that in
and through you I will obtain the blessing and inheritance of eternal life.

31

Isaiah 61:10 *I will greatly rejoice in the Lord, my whole being will exult in my God; for he has clothed me with the garments of salvation, he has covered me with the robe of righteousness, as a bridegroom decks himself with a garland, and as a bride adorns herself with her jewels.*

The hope of Heaven, where I will wear the white robe, sweetens all the bitterness of death. Jesus is with me; he comforts me and sustains me. Holy Redeemer, who has clothed me with the robe of righteousness, clothe me also with the Heavenly robe of joy. I have peace with God through our Lord Jesus Christ. Life and salvation are waiting for me.

John 3:16 *For God so loved the world that he gave his only Son, so that everyone who believes in him may not perish but may have eternal life.*

Holy God, I know that you love me, and gave your Son to die for my sins. I have believed in him, and desire to remain strong in this faith till the last moment of my life. Strengthen me in faith, and grant that what I have believed in this world, I may experience in the world to come. Lord Jesus, keep me in your Holy Presence eternally.

1 Peter 1:18-19 *You know that you were ransomed from the futile ways inherited from your ancestors, not with perishable things like silver or gold, but with the precious blood of Christ, like that of a lamb without defect or blemish.*

Almighty God, I come before you as your child whom you have loved and created. Lamb of God, who takes away the sin of the world, have mercy on me. Do not look upon my sins, but upon the holiness of Jesus which I make my own by faith. Jesus, plead for me; you are my Mediator, Intercessor, and Savior.

Heb. 4:16 *Let us therefore approach the throne of grace with boldness, so that we may receive mercy and find grace to help in time of need.*

Merciful Creator, I lift my eyes to you. I know that in your timing, it is you who will remove my cross; after the storm you will let me see the sun again. I place everything in the hands of the Holy Redeemer; my thoughts, my feelings, my loves, and my possessions. I have experienced true sorrow for my sins and now live immersed in the divine mercy of my loving Savior.

Rev. 21:4 *He will wipe every tear from their eyes. Death will be no more; mourning and crying and pain will be no more, for the first things have passed away.*

Dearest Jesus, I rejoice in anticipation of the hour when, with glorified vision, I will behold your face. There my body will shine as the sun, and my eyes will no more be wet with tears, but filled with light and splendor. In you I will find joy and peace.

Luke 2:29-30 *Master, now you are dismissing your servant in peace, according to your word; for my eyes have seen your salvation.*

The peace of God, which surpasses all understanding, keeps my heart and mind focused on Jesus Christ and eternal life. Gracious God, how sweet are the promises which you have given me in your Word. I ask you to let your Word now, in the hour of my death, comfort me, refresh me, and give me peace.

John 17:24 *Father, I desire that those also, whom you have given me, may be with me where I am, to see my glory, which you have given me because you loved me before the foundation of the world.*

What a joyful and blessed meeting that will be, when I come to you, Lord

Jesus, and behold you face to face. I have loved you here on earth even when I did not see you. How I will delight in you when I come where you are, to the assembly of the saints and elect. How great is your glory! I have not heard in this life the half of what I will see there. Lord Jesus, draw me to you, and prepare me for a joyful entrance into your glory.

Rom. 14:7-8   *We do not live to ourselves, and we do not die to ourselves. If we live, we live to the Lord, and if we die, we die to the Lord; so then, whether we live or whether we die, we are the Lord's.*

Great and Holy God, I have become your own in Holy Baptism. I have remained yours by faith. Let me now in death also be your own. Jesus Christ, Son of God, who has made sufficient atonement for all my sins, and who is my only helper and Comforter, let me hide in your holy wounds. Amen.

2 Tim. 2:8 *Remember Jesus Christ, raised from the dead, a descendant of David—that is my gospel.*

Dearest Jesus, you are deeply engraved in my heart. Your sorrowful passion and death was followed by your Resurrection. You are my hope. Because you live, I also will live. I desire to be with you, now and forever.

Luke 23:42-43 *Then he said, "Jesus, remember me when you come into your kingdom." He replied, "Truly I tell you, today you will be with me in Paradise."*

Dearest Jesus, in the widespread arms of the cross you are ready to embrace sinners, even at the last moments of our lives. Embrace me now with your grace and mercy. Receive into your hands my soul; let it remain in your keeping and enter into the joys of paradise.

I also say with the dying thief: "Lord Jesus, remember me." Remember that I am your child. Let me be with you today in paradise.

Psalm 73:25-26 *Whom have I in heaven but you? And there is nothing on earth I desire other than you. My flesh and my heart may fail, but God is the strength of my heart and my portion forever.*

Most Holy Jesus, my life ebbs away; take me to yourself. My Shepherd, receive your sheep; my Bridegroom, receive your bride; my Parent, receive your child; my Jesus, receive the soul that you have redeemed. This I pray, this I desire; and now I close my eyes.

Luke 23:46 *And Jesus, crying with a loud voice, said, "Father, into your hands I commend my spirit." Having said this, he breathed his last.*

Jesus, my Lord and Redeemer, I now pray in your words: "Father, into your hands I commend my spirit." Your last prayer on the cross will be my last prayer also. Lord Jesus, to you I live, to you I die. Living or dying, I am yours.

2 Peter 3:13 *But, in accordance with his promise, we wait for new heavens and a new earth, where righteousness is at home.*

Heavenly Creator, receive now my soul into your Heavenly Realm. Come, Lord Jesus, I wait for you. Lead me to your everlasting joys. God the Father, what you have created; God the Son, what you have redeemed; God the Holy Spirit, what you have sanctified; this I commend into your hands. To your Holy Name be praise and glory now and forever. Amen.

III: Prayers for the Final Hours

Do not fear, for I have redeemed you;
I have called you by name, you are mine.
—Isaiah 43:1

❖ In my dying hour you alone are my
  salvation, Lord Jesus. Be with me
  when I grow pale in death. Be with
  me when my hearing fails and
  instruct, console, and refresh me
  inwardly in my soul. Be with me
  when my speech leaves me and I am
  no longer able to pray, and pray for
  me then, dear Lord. Holy Spirit of
  God, pray for me and make inter-
  cession for me with groanings which
  cannot be uttered. Be with me, dearest Friend, when I leave this world,
  and lead me to the blessedness of
  Heaven.

❖ Jesus, my Savior and Redeemer, guide
  me from this temporal life to everlasting life. Though the way of death is

dark, I will walk in the light; for you, Lord, are my Light. Stand by my death-bed and receive my soul when it leaves my body. When I close my eyes in death, let my soul behold you. Lead me to Heaven, to the holy angels, and to the assembly of those who have gone before me. Accompany me to the throne of your Heavenly Father, and present me there as one who belongs to you, that I may be received as an heir to eternal life.

❖ Refresh me in my final hour through the consolations of the Holy Spirit, and let me hear joy and gladness. Be with me when my end comes. My death is my entrance to eternal life. There I will find peace, joy, comfort, gladness, light, a white robe, a beautiful crown. There all my sorrows and suffering will end, and I will have rest, happiness, and salvation. Be with me, Good Shepherd, on this journey through death to eternal life. Give

me the joyfulness of faith and the
sweetness of your consolation, that I
may begin and finish my journey
through death happy and blessed.

❖ Dearest Jesus, you have purchased
my soul with your precious blood;
wash and cleanse it, that it may be
pure and well-pleasing to God. As the
end of my earthly life approaches, I
desire to turn my heart and mind and
eyes to you. Lord, if it be your will, let
me hear the words of encouragement
spoken by those who surround me.
Jesus, let me experience the sweetness of your presence, and be
refreshed by the consolations of the
Holy Spirit. Let me calmly and peacefully fall asleep in faith, and remain
united with you before death, in
death, and after death.

❖ Jesus, my heart is filled with sorrow
when I think of the many times I
have offended you throughout my life;

in my thoughts, words, and actions. I ask you to wash me clean from all my sins and to remember them no more. You are my Savior, Mediator, and Intercessor with your Heavenly Father; hear my prayer, and seal forgiveness on my heart through your Holy Spirit.

❖ Lamb of God who takes away the sins of the world, have mercy on me. Jesus, your death is my life. Because you have suffered and died for me, I will not suffer eternal condemnation and death, but will have life through you. God so loved the world that he gave his only-begotten Son, that whoever believes in him will not die, but have everlasting life. By the power of the Holy Spirit, I believe this and trust that death will open the door to eternal life for me.

❖ Because Jesus is crowned with glory and honor, I also will see victory after the conflict, and receive a glorious robe and a beautiful crown from the hand of the Lord. Since I am a child of God, I am also an heir to God's kingdom. I will receive a Heavenly inheritance and be exalted to glory. I willingly unite my suffering with Christ, that I may live and reign with him eternally.

❖ I will remain united with Christ in life, in suffering, and in death. Body and soul may part, but Jesus and my soul will never part. I must leave the world and be separated from my friends, but never from my Lord. Jesus, I have enclosed you in my heart, and there I will hold you in true faith till you bring me to your Heavenly glory. Give me the grace to say: "Lord Jesus, living or dying I am yours."

❖ In Heaven with you, in everlasting joy, there will be no grief or sorrow, no

sickness or pain, no suffering or
death, but all will be joy and happiness, peace, delight, sweetness, light,
and glory eternally. I rejoice in anticipation of that life and glory! There my
Savior will wipe away all tears from
my eyes.

❖ Lamb of God, your death has sweet-
ened my death. I give you ten thousand thanks for all you have done for
me. Your death has reconciled me to
God, and brought me peace, forgiveness of sins, sanctification, and salvation. Because you live, I also will live.
You have acquired Heaven for me and
prepared a mansion for me there.
When my earthly life ends, my heart
ceases to beat, and my body and soul
part. I know that I will go to you, my
Savior.

❖ Since Jesus has risen, God's word
assures me that I also, though I die,
will rise again. On the last day my

body will be raised and will shine like
the sun in the realm of the Creator; it
will be transformed and glorified, and
clothed with white robes. This is a
great consolation to me, and it is so
because Jesus has risen from the
dead. Christ is risen; I also will rise.
Jesus lived; I also will live.

❖ After death I will ascend to Heaven
and be with God in glory. The sheep
will be with the Shepherd, the disci-
ple with the Master, the servant with
the Lord. Jesus, Merciful One, you are
my greatest hope and my sweetest
joy; receive my soul into your realm.

❖ My death journey will lead me from
darkness to light. I will inherit a
place in my Heavenly Creator's home.
I will stand before the throne of God
and see God's face, and this vision will
fill me with inexpressible joy. I will
live in God's presence and be
refreshed by God throughout eternity.

❖ In peace and happiness I will pass away in accordance with the will of God. My heart is content and death is but a sleep. I die joyfully, because my sins are forgiven by the suffering and death of Jesus. I rejoice to depart and be with Christ. I am not afraid because I am going out of the world into Heaven, away from this valley of tears to the place which Christ has prepared for me, a place of happiness that surpasses all human understanding and will last forever.

❖ I reach out my arms toward Jesus to never more let him go. I remember how he extended his two arms upon the cross and died in that position, as though he would embrace me. So I will now die with arms outstretched to embrace Jesus.

Bridegroom of my soul, embrace me, and present me transformed and glorified before your Heavenly Father. What a happy entrance that will be.

These will be my thoughts in death.

❖ Jesus, make my death to be a sweet and gentle slumber, and let me depart in faith and love toward you. Give me rest from my cross, rest from all trouble and sorrow and grief, rest from all pain. When the door of this life closes after me, open to me the door of eternal life. I have directed my thoughts to Heaven here in this life. Open wide the gate of Heaven when I close my earthly pilgrimage.

❖ I am coming from faith to sight. The Creator holds out the crown to me. Jesus takes me by the hand and leads me to eternal happiness. The Holy Spirit adorns me with light and gladness. The holy angels rejoice over my entrance into the Heavenly life of joy. All the elect and saints of God extend a joyous welcome.

*Father, into your hands
I commend my spirit.
To you, almighty God,
be praise and glory to all eternity.
AMEN.*

*Holy, Holy, Holy, Lord God of hosts,
heaven and earth
are filled with your glory,
Hosanna in the highest.
Blessed is the one who comes
in the name of the Lord,
Hosanna in the highest.*

**Be With Me
for Eternity**

Part Two

Reflections of Hope

I. Soul Mates

An old, old man had journeyed for a very long time. His eyes were dim, his glasses shattered, and he could no longer find his way. His weary limbs were almost incapable of carrying him and he knew his journey was nearly over. But now he needed someone to help, comfort, and guide him.

The first person he encountered was a successful young man. When the old man with the tattered coat and unruly hair asked for assistance, the younger man was repulsed by the sight of him. Overcome with fear, the young man refused to acknowledge him and turned away, leaving the old man to continue his journey alone.

The next person the old man approached was a wealthy woman. When he tried to explain his dilemma to her, she didn't want to take the time to listen to where he had been and where he wanted to go. She gave him a few coins, which had no value to him at this point in his journey, and she hastily continued on her way.

By now the sun was setting, darkness was approaching, and the old man felt the chill of the night air. He was all alone. And he was afraid. He staggered on until he came upon a cottage with a warm light coming through the open door. He was welcomed by a wise and gentle old woman who invited him to rest by the fire. He told her about his long journey, his weariness, and the indifference of the people he met along the way. The gentle woman listened to him, understood him, and knew how to help him.

After stirring the fire, the old woman wrapped a warm blanket around his frail body. "There, there," she spoke softly. She continued her work through the long, dark night: "There, there."

By morning the old man was nowhere to be seen. A beautiful young child removed the blanket and ran off into the radiant morning sunshine.

Then the righteous will shine like the sun in the kingdom of their father.
—Matt. 13:43

The setting sun, the approaching darkness, and the chill in the air symbolize the fear and loneliness that dying people can experience as they approach the end of their life. The only place the old man found real comfort, help, and direction was with the wise and gentle woman. She became his soul mate, his spiritual caregiver. The old woman turned to the warm fire and stirred the flames of faith and hope. She wrapped him in a blanket of compassion. Her words of consolation represent prayers of hope and joy, the calm assurance that everything would be all right.

Dying people need and respond to a soul mate. They must feel valued and cared for. They need someone to be with them, someone with whom they can communicate openly and truthfully, someone who cares how they feel about what is happening to them. With loving support, a sense of value, purpose, and direction can be restored, and people can find true meaning in the final days of their lives.

We are to honor the sanctity of health in ourselves and in others, but we are not to let our fear of death get in the way of helping those who are sick and dying. Jesus was the faithful friend of the sick, their adviser and comforter. He went with a helping hand to the bedside of the sick. He lovingly called to himself the blind, the lame, the leper, and the man sick with palsy. As Christians, followers of Jesus, we are called to do the same.

We may not be able to perform miracles, but we can perform acts of kindness! We may not be able to heal the hopelessly sick, or stop death, but we can be with those who are dying in loving support, with a message of hope. We may not be able to get rid of pain, but our words and prayers can bring comfort to those who can no longer enjoy good health. Let Jesus' words not be spoken of us! "I was sick and you did not comfort me."

Those who care for the dying embark on a spiritual journey just as surely as those who are dying. By opening ourselves to the guidance of the Holy Spirit, we caregivers can share in the joy of the soul as it enters Heaven.

As we come to Jesus, the Source of Living Water and the Fountain of Divine Mercy, asking nourishment for the dying, we discover that we also are nourished in the process. Our understanding of life is

deepened, our faith strengthened, and we
grow in trust of the unfathomable love
and divine mercy of God Almighty.

It's about love, and about being com-
pletely present with someone at a very
difficult time. It's about listening to them
and understanding their needs. It's about
sharing a hope that can be trusted, and
about helping them prepare for their
journey. It's about walking with them
along the difficult path, and believing
that Jesus, the Lord of Love and Mercy,
will be waiting to receive them into eternal life.

Everyone has the right and duty to
prepare for the solemn moment of death.
As one prepares to close the door on
earthly life, there are many spiritual
needs. This is a time for forgiveness,
thanksgiving, and farewells to dear ones.
It is a time to let go and to look beyond
the darkness of death. It is a time to
pray for God's mercy and help.

In the light of Christ, the soul can
look with joy and anticipation to a life

that does not end, and to a time when there will be no more suffering and pain. With eyes lifted to Heaven, hearts can be filled with desire to reach out to the Heavenly Creator who calls us home.

By his own example, the Holy Redeemer taught us that the way to prepare for death is to pray. And just as he asked his apostles to stay awake and pray with him, he is calling us to pray with one another when we are about to die, to support one another with faith, compassion, and love. In and through Christ, we will be made perfect. Together, we are called to the foot of the cross for consolation, grace, strength, healing, and mercy by the Holy One who gave his life because he loves us.

Prayer is the language of the soul's yearning for God. It is generally agreed that even though a dying person may no longer be able to speak or respond, that person can still hear. For some, prayers read aloud at their death-bed may be the final opportunity to turn their hearts to

God and to feel the peace of Christ in their souls.

II. Everybody Wants to Go to Heaven, But ...

Everybody wants to go to Heaven, but nobody wants to die. This is life's great paradox. It has been woven into our human nature by the Creator of the Universe, and it's there for a purpose. To understand the paradox frees us to move beyond it.

God gave us the gift of life; our great love and passion for life is implanted deep in our being. Without this passion for life, the continuation of our existence after death would be a matter of indifference to us. It is also that God-given love of life that inspires a natural shrinking from death.

There is, however, an unhealthy fear of death that can be more painful than death itself. It wears out the spirit, weakens the body, and deprives us of all capacity for joy. Those who are always dreading death die a thousand times and suffer each day of their lives.

Death itself is not painful, because it is the end of all pain and sickness. It is like falling into a deep sleep. We are never aware of the moment we actually fall asleep, and it is not a terrible moment for the dying person. Sickness is distressing; but sickness is not death, it only introduces it. You do not see yourself die, just as you do not see yourself fall asleep.

When our hour has come, we will be embraced by the all-loving Father who created us and has singled us out, not for eternal suffering and destruction, but for eternal bliss.

Do not fear, for I have redeemed you; I have called you by name, you are mine. When you pass through the waters, I will be with you; and through the rivers, they will not overwhelm you; when you walk

*through fire you will not be burned, and
the flame will not consume you. For I am
the Lord your God.*

—Isaiah 43:1-3

Death is a transition of life, not an
accident of nature. It is a sacred
moment—the birth of the soul to whole-
ness. It leads to life in abundance, and
reunion with loved ones who have gone
before us.

Jesus assured us that our souls are
immortal, and that after death they will
exist in a higher and happier sphere
which God has prepared for us from the
beginning. He said to his companion on
the cross, "Today you will be with me in
paradise."

The hand that created us loves us,
protects us, and guides us. The Creator
who has blessed our life on earth with
many gifts and joys will not be less gen-
erous when it is our time to enjoy a higher level of existence.

How did our Savior describe death?

He called it, "Going to the Father." What a happy thought to think that our departure from this world is like going to the Father, a union with God. Jesus gave us the assurance of meeting again in eternity. Before he ascended into Heaven, he consoled the disciples who would miss him:

You have pain now; but I will see you again, and your hearts will rejoice, and no one will take your joy from you.
                                        —John 16:22

III. My Journey

The first time I was called to pray with a dying person I was 13 years old. My grandmother telephoned to say that my grandfather, who was dying of cancer, was asking for me to come to his bedside to read the Litany of the Saints to him. I responded without hesitation. Having grown up in a large, Irish Catholic family, I had experienced deaths, funerals, and Irish wakes from a young age, and had accepted death as a part of life. In the years that followed, I said good-bye to many great-aunts and uncles, and two sets of grandparents, as well as some very dear ones who died much too young.

I was well into my adult years when I realized that many people—most people, it seems—are very uncomfortable in the presence of a suffering and dying person; they find it very painful to be there. Yet, dying persons have important needs, and most do not want to be alone.

My own experiences with the deaths of some very dear relatives have played an important role in motivating me to become an advocate for the dying. My great-aunt, Gert, spent the last years of her life in a nursing home. After a time, she lost her vision as well as most of her hearing, and she no longer remembered me or recognized me.

For a while, I stopped visiting her and decided I wanted to remember her as she was in her healthier days.

I was in a Bible study group when it occurred to me that I should not abandon Aunt Gert. I went back to the nursing home to see her. But it was my life that was changed by the experience. Of course she didn't remember me as her niece, but I fed her, comforted her, and talked to her. I continued to do this for some time. Before long it seemed as though I had entered her world, and I became her friend.

Aunt Gert died and I was left with fond memories of a special woman who became a "second grandma" to all of her sister's grandchildren. Some may say the last years of her life were a waste. I disagree. She opened my heart to a greater capacity for compassion. She taught me how to relate to someone whose experience of life is very different from my own, and how love has its own level of communication that extends beyond sight, hearing, and mental capacity. I learned that the living need the dying as much as the dying need the living.

The sudden death of my 20-year-old niece, Julie, had a profound effect on my life. She was a beautiful and bright college student, a highly respected and caring young woman. To lose her was a devastating blow to all who knew and loved her.

Julie needed a serious heart operation and everyone expected a full recovery. It seemed she was on her way back to good health, but things began to turn against her and she became very sick. I was asked to sit with her one afternoon because her parents, who were both teachers, had already spent a lot of time away from their jobs.

I followed an impulse to bring a special book of mediations to comfort Julie, *He and I* by Gabrielle Bossis. I read aloud:

> *You remember how an angel came to stir up the pool for the healing of the sick? No one knew when this would happen. That's*

the way the Spirit comes....Then
wait in the inner stillness; wait
attentively for his coming. Be
like "a garden enclosed."

While I read, Julie listened carefully
to the words, asking me to read them
again. I told her that a friend had given
me the book when I was sick in the hospital, and that I was comforted when my
friend laid her hands on my forehead to
pray for me.

I was already in bed for the night
when we received a call that Julie was
very ill. The doctors didn't know what
was wrong; they had taken tests and
would not know the results for several
days. A voice inside directed me: "Get
dressed and go to the hospital. Julie may
go into a coma; she should not be alone."
I did not understand why, I only knew
what I had to do.

Even though visiting hours were over,
I asked if I could see Julie. When I saw
her I knew I had to stay. The nurse

agreed to let me spend the night. I asked for a cup of coffee and a chair. A short while later Julie woke up for the last time. She knew I was with her. I called a nurse for help. When the nurse took her blood pressure she realized that Julie was critically ill. And, test or no test, they had to fight to save her life. I assured Julie that I would stay with her, and never having done this before, I laid my hands on her forehead and prayed for God's comfort, healing, and blessing.

Later, as I waited outside the intensive care unit, I begged God to help the doctors save her, but things were not getting better and it was time to call a priest. As the priest gave her the Last Rites, Julie went into a coma. The doctors did everything possible to save her, but two days later we lost Julie. I cannot help but recall her mother's words of encouragement, "Honey, through your suffering you are earning a beautiful crown in Heaven." None of us realized how soon she would be wearing that crown.

I was forever changed by this experience. I cannot say why God allowed Julie to be taken from us. But I thank God for the time we had with her. I can tell you that I felt the powerful presence of a loving God when I was with Julie. He was not only calling Julie to be with himself for eternity, but he loved her so much that he extended his loving hand to prepare her and take away her fear as she began the final journey of her soul. The voice that led me to be with Julie was real, and it was important. I believe it was the Holy Spirit.

Five years later, we suffered a second devastating loss on my husband's side of the family. Larry's 33-year-old brother, Ron, had Hodgkin's disease and was undergoing aggressive treatment with a complete recovery in mind. He was a talented television producer and had received national and international awards for his work.

Ron was to be married in four months, and was making plans for the wedding when he became sick with pneumonia. He was put on life support and we were told he was critically ill.

The news was heartbreaking. We were devastated; we could not lose another young person. I had known Ron since he was six years old, and I loved him as a good friend as well as my brother-in-law.

For nine days Ron hovered between life and death. We sat in the waiting room, we prayed, we hoped; we waited for news of a turn-around, but it did not happen. A priest came to give Ron the Last Rites. On his last morning we were able to go into his room to tell him we loved him and to say good-bye. It was a beautiful sunny morning, Mother's Day—the day the angels came to take Ron home.

From Ron's death I learned that there are no guarantees for a long life. From Ron's life I learned that he accomplished as much, and more, in his 33 years than most people do in a long lifetime. His love, talent, loyalty, integrity, and humility are what endeared him to so many people, and those gifts remain as his legacy.

With the death of these two young people I began to feel very vulnerable, as if I were living on borrowed time. Then I realized I am. All of us are. Death comes and we have no say about the when, where, or how. I looked at my own life and could not ignore the call that I heard so clearly with Julie: the invitation to participate in God's holy plan to bring comfort to those who are dying.

Farewell to Grandpa

You were already old when I first met you—
a quiet, gentle, wise old man,
as steady and dependable as the clock
ticking on the dining room wall.
You were from the olden days—
your face and hands showed signs
of years and hard work.
Your eyes and smile shone with
the happiness of a man at peace
with himself and with God.
I will miss you and your old house,
and the walnuts and winter apples,
and all the berries I could eat
on the Fourth of July.
Good-bye Grandpa—your time has come.
As you pass from the Autumn of your life
into the Morning of everlasting glory,
I will remember you with love.

Maureen Rinella, 1976

—for Wendelin Jacob Sohler, 1882-1976

Appendix

Things you can do for someone who is dying:

For physical comfort

☐ Place a cold washcloth on the forehead if the patient is running a fever.

☐ Add or remove blankets as needed.

☐ Raise the head of the bed if it will ease breathing problems.

☐ Moisten a dry mouth with drops of water. A straw with one finger placed over the end can be used to transfer sips of water to the person's mouth.

☐ Be open and sensitive to the needs of the person.

For spiritual comfort

☐ Provide a calm and reassuring presence.

☐ Be a good listener and acknowledge the person's feelings.

☐ Don't hold back your tears. Tears bring healing.

☐ Take time to be quiet. Let God speak

through silence as well as through spoken prayers.

☐ Give reassurance of your presence through gentle strokes, pats, or the holding of a hand, as well as through comforting words.

☐ Encourage reminiscing. When a dying person looks back on his life, help him see God's goodness and grace.

☐ Remind the person that she will be loved and remembered long after she has left this earth.

☐ Reassure the person that death is the door to eternal life. Extend a strong and comforting arm of faith for the dying person to grab hold of if need be.

☐ Help the dying person "get his house in order" if there is unfinished business that keeps him from experiencing peace as death approaches.

☐ Encourage the dying person to forgive others who may have hurt her, recently or long ago. Forgiveness is the road to reconciliation and peace.

☐ Even if a dying person has not been to church in years, he may want to see a chaplain or other person in ministry as death approaches. Offer to help arrange such a meeting if it is the person's wish.

☐ Too often people stay away from a dying loved one because they "want to remember" the way the person looked. In doing so, they miss the opportunity to bring great joy to a dying person. Encourage friends and relatives to make a final visit.

☐ Offer to pray with your loved one regularly. Whether or not you are present physically, you can pray for your loved one. If your loved one is no longer able to pray for herself, pray in her name.

☐ Realize that your presence is your most valuable gift. You are responding to that most basic and urgent prayers of all dying persons:

Be With Me.